DO THE WORK! QUALITY EDUCATION

COMMITTING TO THE UN'S SUSTAINABLE DEVELOPMENT GOALS

JULIE KNUTSON

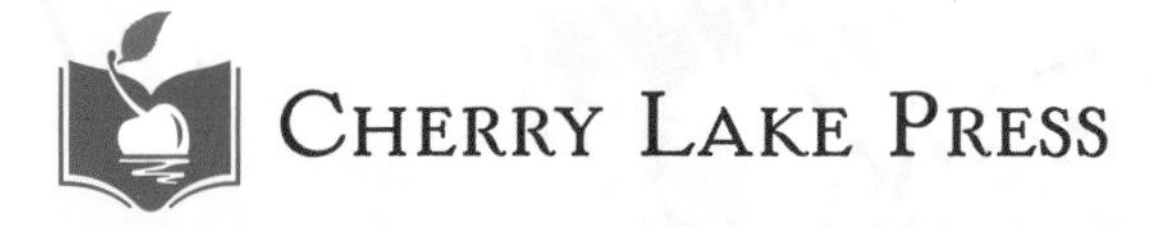

Published in the United States of America by Cherry Lake Publishing Group
Ann Arbor, Michigan
www.cherrylakepublishing.com

Reading Adviser: Beth Walker Gambro, MS, Ed., Reading Consultant, Yorkville, IL
Photo Credits: © Ermolaev Alexander/Shutterstock.com, cover, 1; © De Visu/Shutterstock.com, 5; Infographic From The Sustainable Development Goals Report 2020, by United Nations Department of Economic and Social Affairs © 2020 United Nations. Reprinted with the permission of the United Nations, 7; © Travel Stock/Shutterstock.com, 9; © Richard Juilliart/Shutterstock.com, 10; © Pavel Svoboda Photography/Shutterstock.com, 13; © Tania0378/Shutterstock.com, 14; © greenaperture/Shutterstock.com, 16; © F8 studio/Shutterstock.com, 19; © sirtravelalot/Shutterstock.com, 20; © SeventyFour/Shutterstock.com, 23; © Rey Rodriguez/Shutterstock.com, 24; © fizkes/Shutterstock.com, 27

Cherry Lake Press is an imprint of Cherry Lake Publishing Group.

Library of Congress Cataloging-in-Publication Data
Names: Knutson, Julie, author.
Title: Do the work! : quality education / by Julie Knutson.
Description: Ann Arbor, Michigan : Cherry Lake Publishing, [2022] | Series: Committing to the UN's Sustainable Development Goals | Includes bibliographical references. | Audience: Grades: 4-6
Identifiers: LCCN 2021036396 (print) | LCCN 2021036397 (ebook) | ISBN 9781534199262 (hardcover) | ISBN 9781668900406 (paperback) | ISBN 9781668901847 (pdf) | ISBN 9781668906163 (ebook)
Subjects: LCSH: Sustainable Development Goals–Juvenile literature. | United Nations–Juvenile literature. | Educational equalization–Juvenile literature. | Inclusive education–Juvenile literature. | World citizenship–Juvenile literature.
Classification: LCC LC213 .K48 2022 (print) | LCC LC213 (ebook) | DDC 379.2/6–dc23/eng/20211006
LC record available at https://lccn.loc.gov/2021036396
LC ebook record available at https://lccn.loc.gov/2021036397

Cherry Lake Publishing Group would like to acknowledge the work of the Partnership for 21st Century Learning, a Network of Battelle for Kids. Please visit http://www.battelleforkids.org/networks/p21 for more information.

Printed in the United States of America
Corporate Graphics

ABOUT THE AUTHOR

Julie Knutson is an author-educator who writes extensively about global citizenship and the Sustainable Development Goals. Her previous book, *Global Citizenship: Engage in the Politics of a Changing World* (Nomad Press, 2020), introduces key concepts about 21st-century interconnectedness to middle grade and high school readers. She hopes that this series will inspire young readers to take action and embrace their roles as changemakers in the world.

TABLE OF CONTENTS

CHAPTER 1

Meet the SDGs

Have you ever woke up, pulled the covers over your head, and groaned, "Why do I have to get out of bed and go to school?!" While you might sometimes wish you could stay home and play, time spent in school is incredibly valuable. At school, you develop skills that help you now and in the future. You learn to read, write, and understand how our world works. You work together with peers to solve problems. Education can be a force for promoting global peace, creating a healthier planet, and making life-improving inventions.

The right to a quality education is considered a **fundamental** human right. It is something that *all* people, everywhere on the planet, deserve. But in today's world, not everyone receives an equal education. Across the world, millions of people work to improve education. They are students, teachers, parents, and

Access to a quality education helps people discover their interests and reach their full potential.

community members. They are united by a common goal—to achieve a world in which all people receive a quality education and lifelong learning opportunities. You can join them! Read on to learn how you can help make the **United Nations**' (UN) fourth **Sustainable** Development Goal (SDG), "Quality Education," a reality.

STOP AND THINK: *Think about all the different people who help you learn. Who are they, and what have they taught you? They can be parents, grandparents, neighbors, teachers, or friends. There are so many ways to learn and so many ways to share what you know!*

What Are the SDGs?

In 2015, the UN released the 17 SDGs. The SDGs range from "No Poverty" (SDG 1) to "Reduced Inequalities" (SDG 10) to "Climate Action" (SDG 13). At the core, these 17 goals are about making life better now and in the future, for "people and the planet." All 191 UN member states have agreed to cooperate in reaching the 169 SDG targets by 2030.

"Quality Education" is the fourth goal. The promise? To "ensure **inclusive** and **equitable** quality education and promote lifelong learning opportunities for all." This means making sure that everyone can improve themselves through learning opportunities. It means that all children can enroll in school. It means that everyone can learn to read and write. And it means that when children go to school, they know the environment will be safe and free from discrimination.

4 QUALITY EDUCATION

ENSURE INCLUSIVE AND EQUITABLE QUALITY EDUCATION AND PROMOTE LIFELONG LEARNING OPPORTUNITIES FOR ALL

BEFORE COVID-19

PROGRESS TOWARDS INCLUSIVE AND EQUITABLE QUALITY EDUCATION WAS **TOO SLOW**

OVER 200 MILLION CHILDREN WILL STILL BE **OUT OF SCHOOL** IN 2030

COVID-19 IMPLICATIONS

SCHOOL CLOSURES KEPT **90% OF ALL STUDENTS OUT OF SCHOOL** REVERSING YEARS OF PROGRESS ON EDUCATION

INEQUALITIES IN EDUCATION ARE EXACERBATED BY COVID-19

IN LOW-INCOME COUNTRIES, CHILDREN'S SCHOOL COMPLETION RATE IS

79% IN RICHEST 20% OF HOUSEHOLDS

34% IN POOREST 20% OF HOUSEHOLDS

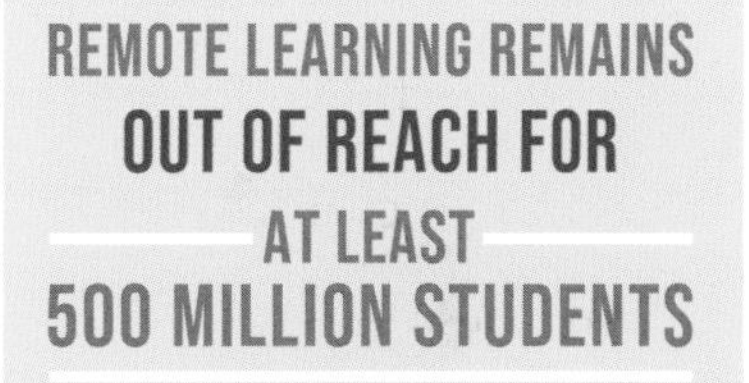

ONLY **65%** OF **PRIMARY SCHOOLS** HAVE BASIC HANDWASHING FACILITIES CRITICAL FOR COVID-19 PREVENTION

ACCESS MORE DATA AND INFORMATION ON THE INDICATORS AT HTTPS://UNSTATS.UN.ORG/SDGS/REPORT/2020/

Related Goals

As you look at the full list of SDGs, you'll notice a lot of overlap between goals. Working to improve education increases the opportunities available to people worldwide. It can lift people out of poverty and create opportunities for women and girls. People with a well-rounded education can achieve their full potential. They can help solve other problems that threaten our world, including climate change.

Ready to help make SDG 4 a reality? Read on to learn more about what's being done—and about what *you* can do—to create quality educational opportunities for people worldwide.

Education is an essential human right.

Globally, around 129 million girls are out of school.

Edutainment, anyone?

For years, TV shows like *Sesame Street*, *Daniel Tiger*, and *Sid the Science Kid* have introduced young children to concepts such as identifying shapes and expressing emotions. In 2013, a **social business** in Tanzania called Ubongo Learning set out to do the same. Ubongo introduces core math and literacy skills to **pan-African** audiences through fun, educational cartoons.

The organization, whose name means "brain" in the **Kiswahili** language, was founded to address the challenge of providing quality early childhood education to children in Africa. According to the UN, less "than one half of schools in **sub-Saharan** Africa have access to drinking water, electricity, computers and the internet." Ubongo allows children to learn through media that might be more accessible at home, like television, radio, and cell phones.

So how are Ubongo's efforts to improve education going? Children who viewed the network's best-known show, *Akili and Me*, were better prepared for elementary math and reading tasks than peers who didn't watch the show. Ubongo's programs are available in 9 languages and are currently viewed in 41 countries across the world!

CHAPTER 2

Why Do We Have Goals?

Consider these examples. Luis is in fifth grade. He loves manga and anime. He wants to learn Japanese so that he can watch his favorite movies without subtitles. Anya is in fourth grade. She'd love to learn how to play guitar, but has no idea where to start.

What's the best way for these kids to reach their goals?

Rather than just grabbing a dictionary or plucking at strings, Luis and Anya can make step-by-step plans to reach their goals. The acronym "SMART," which stands for Specific, Measurable, Achievable, Relevant, and Timed, can guide them in the process. This process for setting goals isn't used only by individuals. It's also used by large organizations like the UN to form a plan for meeting the SDGs.

Many children in rural areas walk to school. Depending on how far they have to travel, the terrain can be dangerous.

Schools should be safe places. But if they lack hand washing stations, they are vulernable to health threats like COVID-19.

STOP AND THINK: *What goals do you have? How could you use the SMART strategy to reach them?*

SDG 4 breaks down into eight smaller targets. Think of these targets as the stepping stones on the path to achieving quality education. All of them need to be firmly placed in the ground to meet the goal. Those targets are:

- Free education.
- Equal access to quality pre-K education.
- Equal access to **technical** and higher education.
- Increase the number of people with the skills needed for financial security.
- End all discrimination in education.
- Achieve universal literacy and **numeracy**.
- Education for sustainable development and global citizenship.
- Build and upgrade inclusive and safe schools.

In the beginning of 2020, students had to adapt quickly to remote learning.

But the UN didn't stop at setting targets for SDG 4. Specific, measurable **indicators** track progress on each point. People can act on these indicators to achieve results. Read more to learn about actions that you can take—at home, at school, and in the larger world—to help!

In recent years, much progress has been made to improve access to education. According to the UN, 70 percent of children completed elementary school in 2000. By 2019, that number was 85 percent. But in 2020, the COVID-19 pandemic threatened to upset many of these gains. The COVID crisis kept 1.6 billion learners home, in every corner of the world. Many experts predict that many students won't return to school. Others may lose some of their academic skills.

CHAPTER 3

Do the Work! Contribute to the Goals at Home

How can you and your family contribute to the goal of "Quality Education?" Educating yourself doesn't need to be limited to school hours. Learn about issues that spark your curiosity and passion. Share your knowledge with others, and act on it!

- **Educate** — Use what you learn at school to educate the people in your life! In the process, you'll not just help with SDG 4, but also with other SDGs, such as "Climate Action." For example, researchers at North Carolina State University in 2019 found that 10- to 14-year-old kids who studied climate change at school could reshape their parents' attitudes about the subject.

STOP AND THINK: *Do you talk with the adults in your life about issues that concern you? How can you make sure that these conversations are respectful and factual?*

Share what you learn with friends.

Books are expensive. In the United States, two-thirds of children living in poverty have no books to call their own.

- **Donate** — If you have books that you've outgrown, donate them! Many libraries have sections where gently used books can find new homes. The profit from any sale goes to support library programming. You can also donate books to other local charities like Goodwill Industries, which provides job training services for adults. In cities around the country, local literacy groups like Philadelphia's Reading Recycled "strive to eliminate children growing up without books in their homes." Research to see if similar organizations exist in your city or town.
- **Take Field Trips** — We can learn a lot from the people and places around us. Whether at your local library, neighborhood historic sites, or nature preserves, get out and explore. Ask questions about the past, present, and future of your community. Think about ways that you can make it better for *all* of your neighbors.

Do the Work! Contribute to the Goals at School

What better place to advocate for quality education than at school? You and your peers can do this in a number of ways. Push for global citizenship and sustainability education. Use your school library as a resource to create community conversations. Call out injustice and inequality when and where you see it. Raise awareness. And always ask questions!

- **Raise Awareness** — At school, you can educate faculty and classmates about all 17 SDGs. Together, you can decide on what SDGs to tackle as a community and how to do it. You can also tell your teachers and administrators about global citizenship and sustainability education programs. If students create demand for content through positive conversations, petitions, and editorials in the school newspaper, decision-makers will likely pay attention!

Use your school library as a resource to create community conversations.

According to the Little Free Library, more than 30 million American adults cannot read above a third-grade level.

- **Fundraise** — You and your peers can host car washes, craft sales, walk/runs, and other fundraisers to push for the goal of quality education for all. Use the money you raise to support local literacy organizations or global groups that work for equality in education. You could also raise funds to build a Little Free Library on your school's playground.
- **Start a Book Club** — Chances are your teacher or school librarian would be willing to help you start a book club. Book clubs can be a great way to explore the various SDGs, both through fiction and nonfiction. You can host book talks to share what you learn and discuss with other members of the school community too!

STOP AND THINK: *Are there other types of programs or clubs that you could launch at your school to promote SDG 4? If so, what are they?*

CHAPTER 5

Do the Work! Contribute to the Goals in Your Community

Not everyone receives equal access to quality, current resources or supportive and encouraging teachers. In U.S. schools, Black children often face harsher punishments and higher suspension rates than their White peers. This suggests **bias** and racial discrimination in these schools. Other factors, including poverty, also create unequal opportunities. Think about school closures during COVID-19. Students who had high-speed internet access likely experienced fewer learning disruptions than those with no or unstable home internet.

- **Learn and Advocate** — Learn about educational challenges in your community. Do all schools get equitable resources? Are free pre-K programs available to families with young children? Are stories of all people and groups represented

All students faced learning loss during the COVID-19 pandemic, but students of color were mostly affected.

in the classroom? If the answers to these questions are not "yes," ask "why?" Continue asking until you find the root causes. Then start thinking about solutions. Write to leaders such as school administrators and school board officials about any concerns that you have.

- **Volunteer** — Youths and teens are welcome volunteers at many community organizations that promote quality education.

- **Encourage** — Remember to say "thank you" to the educators in your life! A word of gratitude to teachers, tutors, mentors, and librarians can mean a lot, especially when it comes from the people whose lives they directly affect.

Malala and the Fight for Educational Equality for Girls

Malala Yousafzai is perhaps the world's best-known advocate for quality education. When Malala was a child growing up in Pakistan's Swat Valley, a religious group called the Taliban banned girls from attending school. Malala and her family valued education. As she recalls in her **memoir**, *I Am Malala*, her father "believed that lack of education was at the root of all Pakistan's problems." She explains that in his view, "Ignorance allowed politicians to fool people and bad administrators to be reelected. He felt schooling should be available for all, rich and poor, boys and girls." Malala continued to attend school and became an activist for the right to education.

Malala became well known. She wrote blogs that people read around the world. A documentary was made about her life. In 2012, while riding the bus home from school, she was shot in a failed **assassination** attempt. But Malala didn't give up. After her recovery, she spoke up even more for girls' rights to education. In October 2014, she became the youngest person in history to win the Nobel Peace Prize.

Extend Your Learning

Background

Chapter 4 presented the idea of starting a Sustainable Development Goals book club at your school. The UN provides support for students and teachers wanting to launch book clubs, including reading lists and tips for getting started. To learn more, visit the UN's website or search #SDGBookClub on social media!

Act

The UN offers these tips for starting an SDG book club:

- Start a booklist.
- Invite friends and peers to join.
- Work together to make rules for discussion.
- Decide when and where to meet, whether in person or online.
- Make a to-do list.
- Share what you learned and discussed.

Further Research

BOOKS

Brown, Dinah. *Who Is Malala Yousafzai?* New York, NY: Penguin Young Readers Group, 2015.

Schwab, Christine. *Kids Speak Out About Education.* Vero Beach, FL: Rourke Educational Media, 2020.

WEBSITES

Goal 4: Quality Education—United Nations Sustainable Development
https://www.un.org/sustainabledevelopment/education
Check out the UN's Sustainable Development Goals website for more information on Goal 4.

The Global Goals of Sustainable Development
margreetdeheer.com/eng/globalgoals.html
Check out these free comics about the UN's Sustainable Development Goals.

Why Was School Created?—Wonderopolis
wonderopolis.org/wonder/why-was-school-created
Learn about the first schools.

Glossary

assassination (uh-sah-suh-NAY-shuhn) murder for political or religious reasons

bias (BYE-uhss) prejudice against a group

equitable (EH-kwuh-tuh-buhl) fairness in distributing opportunities and resources

fundamental (fuhn-duh-MEN-tuhl) something that is essential

inclusive (in-KLOO-siv) open to everyone

indicators (in-duh-KAY-tuhrs) measurements of progress

Kiswahili (kih-swah-HEE-lee) another word for Swahili, a language widely spoken in East Africa

memoir (MEM-wahr) a written account of a person's life

numeracy (NOO-muh-ruh-see) having to do with numbers and counting

pan-African (pan-AH-frih-kuhn) across Africa

social business (SOH-shuhl BIZ-nuhss) a business that puts solving social problems and helping people ahead of earning a profit

sub-Saharan (sub-suh-HAIR-uhn) part of Africa south of the Sahara Desert

sustainable (suh-STAY-nuh-buhl) able to be maintained at a certain rate

technical (TEK-nih-kuhl) related to a particular subject

United Nations (yuh-NYE-tuhd NAY-shuhns) the international organization that promotes peace and cooperation among nations

INDEX